# First World War
and Army of Occupation
# War Diary
France, Belgium and Germany

34 DIVISION
102 Infantry Brigade
Northumberland Fusiliers
25th Battalion (Tyneside Irish)
1 February 1918 - 30 April 1919

WO95/2463/3

The Naval & Military Press Ltd
www.nmarchive.com
Published in association with The National Archives

Published by

## The Naval & Military Press Ltd

Unit 10 Ridgewood Industrial Park,

Uckfield, East Sussex,

TN22 5QE England

Tel: +44 (0) 1825 749494

www.naval-military-press.com

www.nmarchive.com

*This diary has been reprinted in facsimile from the original. Any imperfections are inevitably reproduced and the quality may fall short of modern type and cartographic standards.*

**© Crown Copyright**
**Images reproduced by permission of The National Archives, London, England, 2015.**

# Contents

| Document type | Place/Title | Date From | Date To |
|---|---|---|---|
| Heading | WO95/2463 34 Division 102 Infantry Brigade 25 Battalion Northumberland Fusiliers Feb 1918-April 1919 | | |
| Heading | 34 Div 102 Bde 25 North Fus 1918 Feb to 1919 Apl From 103 Bde | | |
| War Diary | Brigade in Resv. | 01/02/1918 | 05/02/1918 |
| War Diary | Durham Lines. | 06/02/1918 | 08/02/1918 |
| War Diary | Blairville | 09/02/1918 | 09/02/1918 |
| War Diary | Gouy | 10/02/1918 | 10/02/1918 |
| War Diary | Ambrines | 11/02/1918 | 28/02/1918 |
| Heading | 34th Division. 102nd Infantry Brigade. War Diary 25th Battalion Northumberland Fusiliers March 1918 | | |
| Heading | War Diary Units 102nd Infantry Brigade 25th N.F. March 1918 Vol 27 | | |
| War Diary | Brigade in Reserve | 01/03/1918 | 01/03/1918 |
| War Diary | Ervillers | 02/03/1918 | 07/03/1918 |
| War Diary | Inniskilling Camp | 08/03/1918 | 08/03/1918 |
| War Diary | Ervillers | 09/03/1918 | 11/03/1918 |
| War Diary | Brigade in Reserve. | 12/03/1918 | 19/03/1918 |
| War Diary | Battn in Support | 20/03/1918 | 31/03/1918 |
| Miscellaneous | Daily Report by Capt. T. McLachlan, M.C., 25th Bn., Northumberland Fusiliers, of operations on March 21st, 32nd and 23rd 1918. | 21/03/1918 | 21/03/1918 |
| Heading | 34th Division. 102nd Infantry Brigade. War Diary 25th Battalion Northumberland Fusiliers April 1918 | | |
| War Diary | Erquinghem Brigade in Reserve | 01/04/1918 | 05/04/1918 |
| War Diary | Houplines in Trenches | 06/04/1918 | 11/04/1918 |
| War Diary | In The Trenches | 11/04/1918 | 11/04/1918 |
| War Diary | In Trenches North of Nieppe | 12/04/1918 | 14/04/1918 |
| War Diary | In Trenches North of Bailleul | 15/04/1918 | 20/04/1918 |
| War Diary | Croix-De-Poperinghe | 21/04/1918 | 22/04/1918 |
| War Diary | San-Jans-Ter-Biezen | 23/04/1918 | 26/04/1918 |
| War Diary | Poperinghe Army Line | 27/04/1918 | 30/04/1918 |
| Heading | 102nd Brigade. 34th Division. War Diary 25th Northumberland Fusiliers May 1918 | | |
| War Diary | Poperinghe Army Line Left Sub Sector | 01/05/1918 | 05/05/1918 |
| War Diary | L.7.b.1.9. 1 Mile East of Sans. Lans-Br Biezen | 06/05/1918 | 06/05/1918 |
| War Diary | L.7.b.1.9. East of Sanjans-Br. Biezen | 07/05/1918 | 10/05/1918 |
| War Diary | L.7.b.1.9. I mile East of San Jans Ter Biezen | 11/05/1918 | 12/05/1918 |
| War Diary | Rubrouck | 13/05/1918 | 13/05/1918 |
| War Diary | Verval | 14/05/1918 | 18/05/1918 |
| War Diary | La Calique | 19/05/1918 | 31/05/1918 |
| Heading | 102nd Brigade. 34th Division. Battalion transferred to 39th Division 17.6.18 War Diary 25th Northumberland Fusiliers June 1918 | | |
| War Diary | La Calique | 01/06/1918 | 10/06/1918 |
| War Diary | Le Wast | 11/06/1918 | 30/06/1918 |
| War Diary | Alquines | 01/07/1918 | 18/07/1918 |
| War Diary | Chelers | 19/07/1918 | 31/07/1918 |
| Miscellaneous | 309th Infantry, A.E.F. France, June 29, 1918. | 29/06/1918 | 29/06/1918 |

| | | | |
|---|---|---|---|
| Miscellaneous | 309th Infantry A.E.F. France, July 5. 18 | 05/07/1918 | 05/07/1918 |
| Miscellaneous | 309th Infantry, A.E.F., France, 13 July 1918 | 13/07/1918 | 13/07/1918 |
| Miscellaneous | Headquarters, 309th Infantry, A.E.F., France, July 20th, 1918. | 20/07/1918 | 20/07/1918 |
| Heading | War Diary of 25th Battn Northumd Fus. From Aug 1st 1918 To Aug 31st 1918 Vol No Vol 32 | | |
| War Diary | Chelers | 01/08/1918 | 04/08/1918 |
| War Diary | Licques | 05/08/1918 | 15/08/1918 |
| War Diary | Abancourt | 23/08/1918 | 23/08/1918 |
| War Diary | Haudricourt | 24/08/1918 | 31/08/1918 |
| Heading | War Diary of 25th Bn. Northumberland Fusiliers. From 1st. September 1918. to 30th. September 1918 | | |
| War Diary | Haudricourt | 01/09/1918 | 30/09/1918 |
| Heading | War Diary. of 25th Bn. Northumberland Fusiliers. From 1st. October, 1918 To 31st. October, 1918 | | |
| War Diary | Haudricourt | 01/10/1918 | 24/10/1918 |
| Heading | War Diary of 25th. Bn. Northumberland Fusiliers. From-1st. Novr, 1918. To-30th Novr. 1918. (Volume XXI). | | |
| War Diary | Haudricourt | 01/11/1918 | 30/11/1918 |
| Heading | Training Cadre 39th Division Divl Troops 25th Bn North'd Fus. Jan-Apr 1919 | | |
| War Diary | Havre | 01/01/1919 | 31/01/1919 |
| War Diary | Havre | 13/01/1919 | 29/01/1919 |
| Miscellaneous | Headquarters 116th Infantry Brigade | 28/02/1919 | 28/02/1919 |
| War Diary | Havre | 01/02/1919 | 28/02/1919 |
| War Diary | Havre | 12/02/1919 | 19/02/1919 |
| War Diary | Havre | 01/03/1919 | 31/03/1919 |
| War Diary | Havre | 14/03/1919 | 14/03/1919 |
| War Diary | Havre | 01/04/1919 | 30/04/1919 |

(3)

WO 95/2463

34 Division
103 Infantry Brigade
25 Battalion Northumberland
Fusiliers
Feb 1918 - April 1919

BEF

34 DIV

102 BDE

25 NORTH FUS

1918 FEB to 1919 APL ~~1919 JUNE~~

~~To 66 DIV 1917 Poole~~

From 103 BDE

25 NF
Volume 26

Army Form C. 2118.

# WAR DIARY
## INTELLIGENCE SUMMARY.
(Erase heading not required.)

| Place | Date | Hour | Summary of Events and Information | Remarks and references to Appendices |
|---|---|---|---|---|
| Brigade in Reserve | Feb 1st | | Baths in rooky commenced having according to Brigade Programme | |
| | | 9am to 10am | Physical drill and Bayonet fighting (all Companies) | |
| | | 10am to 12noon | A.Coy. Range. B.C.&D. Coy. Drill | |
| | | 12.15pm—1pm | Ceremonial drill | |
| | | 2.15pm to 3pm | W.O's and N.C.O's Guard Interiate under I.S.M. | |
| | Feb 2nd | | Training and preparing for preservation day. | |
| | Feb 3rd | | Baths as transferred to the 102nd Infantry Brigade (grenade Supply) and moves to the 102nd Brigade area at DURHAM LINES, Brieux-au-Mont. | |
| | Feb 4th | | Companies are at disposal of Coy Commanders for cleaning up, a proportion of the Baths going to the Baths. | |
| | | 2.30 pm | 2 Officers & S.O.O.R. per Coy were provided for working parties in the Forward Area. | |
| | Feb 5th | 9am to 12pm | Bayonet fighting, Musketry and Coy drill. | |
| | | 2.30 pm | 2 Officers & S.O.O.R. per Coy provided for working party in the Forward Area. | |

**WAR DIARY**
or
**INTELLIGENCE SUMMARY.**
(Erase heading not required.)

Army Form C. 2118.

| Place | Date | Hour | Summary of Events and Information | Remarks and references to Appendices |
|---|---|---|---|---|
| DURHAM LINES. | Feb. 6th | | Bath. Remainder training according to Training Programme. | |
| | | 9 A.m. - 10 a.m. | Physical drill, Bayonet fighting. | |
| | | 10 a.m. - 11 a.m. | Musketry. Platoon drill. All ranks of A. Coy and | |
| | | | about two platoons fire the Lewis Gun. | |
| | | 11 a.m. - 12 Noon. | Company drill. A. Coy. Lewis Gun Range. | |
| | | 2 p.m. - 4.30 p.m. | All available men at work on Aircraft Defences. | A.W.O |
| | Feb. 7th | | Training as per previous day. B. Coy. Lewis Gun Range. Work on Aircraft Defences. | A.W.O |
| | Feb. 8th | | as. | A.W.O |
| BLAIRVILLE | Feb. 9th | | Batln moved to N.O. 4 Camp BLAIRVILLE, arriving there 1 p.m. | A.W.O |
| GOUY | Feb. 10th | | Batln moved to GOUY arriving there at 6.12 Noon. | A.W.O |
| AMBRINES | " 11th | | Batln continued its march and reached the H.Q. Rest Area, AMBRINES. | A.W.O |
| | | at 1 p.m. | | |
| | " 12th | | Coys at the disposal of Coy Commanders for cleaning up &c. Battalion commenced training according to Training Programme. | A.W.O |
| | 13 | 9 a.m. - 12 Noon. | A. & B. Coys. by platoons, Physical Training and Bayonet fighting, Bathing and Wiring. C. & D. Coys on Range. | A.W.O |

# WAR DIARY
## or
## INTELLIGENCE SUMMARY.

*(Erase heading not required.)*

Army Form C. 2118.

| Place | Date | Hour | Summary of Events and Information | Remarks and references to Appendices |
|---|---|---|---|---|
| AMBRINES | 16/15 | | (cont'd) | |
| | | 12.15pm to 1pm | Ceremonial Drill (1 Battalion) | A66D |
| | -14 | 9am to 12 noon | C & D Coys - By platoons, anti-gas Instructions, Bombing & Wiring | A66C |
| | | " | A & B Coys. On Range | |
| | | 12 noon to 1pm | Ceremonial Drill (1 Battalion) | |
| | "15" | 9am to 10am | C & D Coys. Physical Training & Bayonet Fighting | |
| | | " | A & B do. Close order drill | |
| | | 10am to 11am | do. Physical Training & Bayonet Fighting | |
| | | " | C & D Coys. Close order drill | |
| | | 11am to 12 noon | All Coys. Attack in the open. 12.15 to 1pm. Baths Ceremonial Drill. | A66E |
| | "16" | 9am to 10am | A & B Coys Physical Training & Bayonet Fighting. C & D Coys Close order Drill | |
| | | 10am to 11am | do. Coy Drill | |
| | | 11am to 12 noon | do. Close order drill | |
| | | 12.30pm to 1pm | Baths. Ceremonial Drill | |
| | "17" | 10.15am | Church Parade. 2.30pm. A Proportion of the Baths. 5 to 7. The Baths. | A66F |
| | "18" | 9am to 12 noon | A Coy. Attack on Strong Point in accordance with T.S. 32/43 m | A66G |
| | | do. | B Coy. on 'A' Range. C & D. Company in attack. 12 noon to 1pm. Baths Drill | A66H |

Army Form C. 2118.

# WAR DIARY
## or
## INTELLIGENCE SUMMARY.
*(Erase heading not required.)*

Instructions regarding War Diaries and Intelligence Summaries are contained in F. S. Regs., Part II. and the Staff Manual respectively. Title pages will be prepared in manuscript.

| Place | Date | Hour | Summary of Events and Information | Remarks and references to Appendices |
|---|---|---|---|---|
| AMBRINES | Feb 19 | 9 am to 12 noon | Training as yesterday | |
| | | 2.30 pm | W/O's & N.C.O's parade under the Commanding Officer. Lewis Gunners parade for Instruction. Sgn. Lecture by the Commanding Officer. | P.S.O. |
| | Feb 20 | 9 am - 12 noon | A+C Coys Range. C Coy musketry. Bombing. Close order drill | P.S.O. |
| | | 12 noon/5 pm | Battalion drill | |
| | | 3 pm | Lewis Gun inspection by G.O.C. 102nd Infantry Brigade | |
| | 21 | 9 am to 12 noon | A.B.+C. Coys Range. C Coy. Attack Practice. Bombing. P.+B.J. | P.S.O. |
| | | 12 noon to 1 pm | Battalion drill | |
| | 22 | 9 am to 12 noon | Baths in the Attack (All Coys) | |
| | | 12 noon/5 1pm | Bath drill | |
| | | 2.30 pm | Tactical exercise for Officers | P.S.O. |
| | 23 | 9 am | Baths parade on the Parade Ground | |
| | | 9.30 | Commanding Officers parade | |
| | 24 | 10.15 am | Church Parade | P.S.O. |
| | | 9 am | Bath Parade. "Fallering on the Best of the Drum." | P.S.O. |
| | 25 | 9.20 am | Bath marches to "C" Area to carry out an "Attack in the Open" | |

# WAR DIARY
## or
## INTELLIGENCE SUMMARY.
*(Erase heading not required.)*

Army Form C. 2118.

| Place | Date | Hour | Summary of Events and Information | Remarks and references to Appendices |
|---|---|---|---|---|
| AMBRINES | Feb 25 | | (cont.) accordance with Scheme No.1. | |
| | | 2.30 p.m. | Lecture/Salute for Officers N.C.O's provisionarily Ceremonial | App.C. |
| | Feb 26 | 9 a.m. – 10.30 a.m. | Platoon Drill, Bombing. | |
| | | 10.30 a.m. – 1 p.m. | Coys at disposal of Coy Commanders for cleaning up. | |
| | | 2.30 p.m. | The Coy Commanders Inspection of the Battalion. The Battn with other Battns of the Brigade paraded in Close Formation on the Fortune Ground west of AMBRINES | App.D |
| | Feb 27 | | The Battn paraded at 6.20 a.m. and moved by March Route to BERLES-au-BOIS, arriving there about 2 p.m. Battn was billeted there for the night. | |
| | Feb 28 | | The Battn paraded at 6.30 a.m. and moved by march route to ERVILLERS arriving there 2.30 p.m. and occupied ENNISKILLING CAMP. A reconnoitring Party consisting of 11 Officers and Y.O.R. proceeded from BERLES-au-BOIS by Motor Bus to MORY, from where they proceeded to reconnoitre the Right Section, Centre Sector VI. Corps Front, held by the 176th Infantry Brigade. | |

A Lt. Col.
Commanding
25th York & Lanc

34th Division.
102nd Infantry Brigade.

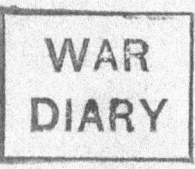

25th BATTALION

NORTHUMBERLAND FUSILIERS

MARCH 1 9 1 8

25ᵀᴴ N.F.

MARCH 1918

**Army Form C. 2118.**

25th N.F.

# WAR DIARY
## or
## INTELLIGENCE SUMMARY.
*(Erase heading not required.)*

Instructions regarding War Diaries and Intelligence Summaries are contained in F. S. Regs., Part II. and the Staff Manual respectively. Title pages will be prepared in manuscript.

| Place | Date | Hour | Summary of Events and Information | Remarks and references to Appendices |
|---|---|---|---|---|
| Brigade in Reserve ERVILLERS | 1/3/18 | | The Battn: Paraded at the disposal of O.C. Sherwood Foresters, Rifle Grenadier, Lewis Gunner, Signallers & Section own instructors. | |
| | 2/3/18 | | The Battn relieved the 2/5th SHERWOOD FORESTERS in the left sub-section, Right Sector, Eastern Sector of the VI Corps front on the night of 2/3 march. Disposition of companies as follows: D Coy right front, B Coy left front, A Coy support, C Coy Reserve | |
| | 3/3/18 | | |  |
| | 4/3/18 | | Reserve for this Junior Intn. relieved | |
| | 5/3/18 | | | |
| | 6/3/18 | | | |
| | 7/3/18 | | Battn was relieved by the 9th Bn. North'd Fusiliers on the night of 7/8th march. | |
| INNISKILLIN CAMP ERVILLERS | 8/3/18 | | Battn. Barracks at the disposal of O.C. Companies. | |
| | 9/3/18 | | | |
| | 10/3/18 | | Officers reconnoitring the third system of defences. The Bn prepared to move (m.m?) fourties for meeting Battn. assembly positions in the forward area | |
| | 11/3/18 | | Bullets moved to positions assembly left behind | |
| BRIGADE in Reserve | 12/3/18 | | The Battn (two Coys) relieved Coys aged on the forward area | |
| " " | 13/3/18 | | Battn. Parades Gun instruction. Remainder I Co'day the boys were used & work making billets. 250 men working hrs of under brigade Instructor. Lewis Gunner, Rifle Grenadier & men on various duties | |
| " " | 14/3/18 | | Battn. Parades Gun instructions. Remainder & men employed on making billets for special instruction. Remainder & men working party. 250 men working party. | |

# WAR DIARY
## or
## INTELLIGENCE SUMMARY.
*(Erase heading not required.)*

Army Form C. 2118.

Instructions regarding War Diaries and Intelligence Summaries are contained in F. S. Regs., Part II. and the Staff Manual respectively. Title pages will be prepared in manuscript.

| Place | Date | Hour | Summary of Events and Information | Remarks and references to Appendices |
|---|---|---|---|---|
| Brigade in Reserve | 15/3/15 | | Battn Parade, Gun & Rifle inspection. Remainder of men employed & mending tables. 250 men working party under Brigade orders. Gas Drill. | |
| " | 16/3/15 | | Parade of Gun & Rifle inspection. Remainder of men working tables. 250 working party. Gas Drill. | |
| " | 17/4/15 | | Battn Parade. Gun & Rifle inspection. Gas Drill. Remainder of men working tables. | |
| " | 18/3/15 | | 250 working party march via Brigade. | |
| " | 19/3/15 | | Battn Parade. Gun & Rifle inspection. Men working on tables. Battn in support to the 9th Bn Northumberland Fusiliers as Battn in support & the | |
| " | 19/3/15 | | Battn relieved the 9 & 13 Northumberland as Battn in support. | |
| Battn in Support | 20/3/15 | | Brigade Artillery manoeuvres the day. By night own Artillery had been in total the nig 6%. | |
| | | | Ref attached whole by May & J McLachlan M.C. | |
| | 21/3/15 | | The Battn were returned by the 92nd Brigade 31st Div. and marched XABLAINZEVILLE. | |
| | 22/3/15 | | The Battn marched X BAILLEULMONT. | |
| | 23/3/15 | | The Battn marched & DENIER | |
| | 24/3/15 | | The Battn marched X VILLES L'HOPITAL. | |
| | 25/3/15 | | The Battn marched X PREVENT and entrained | |
| | 26/3/15 | | The Battn marched by train X STEENBECQUE. & marched X HAVERSQU | |
| | 27/3/15 | | The Battn marched X CARESCURE. | |
| | 28/3/15 | | The Battn marched T ESTAIRE. | |
| | 29/3/15 | | The Battn marched X ERQUINGHEM. | |

DIARY REPORT by CAPT. T. McLACHLAN, M.C.,
25th Bn., Northumberland Fusiliers, of
operations on March 21st, 22nd and 23rd
1918.

On the night of March 21st/22nd 1918 my Company were occupying a position from U.25.a.50.55 to U.19.c.10.80 in the Reserve Battalion sector with the 102nd Brigade.

At about 4-30 a.m. on the morning of the 21st a heavy enemy bombardment opened. The shells employed consisted largely of gas mixed with high explosive. This bombardment lasted for roughly 4 hours. After this period a slight lull for about 20 minutes took place, and the enemy bombardment recommenced this time many more H.E. shells being used.

At roughly about 11-30 a.m. I received an order from Batt. H.Q. to be prepared to counter attack on Tiger trench at U.20.d.10.00. About an hour later I received a second order to form a defensive flank on the right at U.25.d. with my left resting on Pelican Avenue. In pursuance of this order I sent two platoons under 2/Lt. Bowmer along Bunhill Row in the direction of Leg Lane and I myself took two platoons along the road from U.25.a.50.80. to U.25.central. On reaching the point where the 100 contour crosses this road masses of the enemy, several Battalions strong, were seen on Ecoust Spur within 300 to 500 yards in our right rear about the junction of the squares T.U.B. and C. and advancing in North westerly direction. At this point we were subjected to very heavy rifle and machine gun fire from the enemy on the spur, many casualties being inflicted on my force. I thereupon withdrew in a North Westerly direction, parallel to the Railway embankment, and North East of this embankment, throwing out a loose defensive right flank. This I did with a view to preventing an enemy encircling movement from my right.

On reaching the trench running from T.24.b.10.20 southwards I made an attempt to man it, reinforced by men of "A" Coy. 2/Lt. Vipond, O.C. "A" Coy., joining me here, but found the enemy still advancing on my flank. I thereupon threw out a right flank in the direction of the windmill at T.24.d.15.43., placing a strong post on the windmill mound. This position however became untenable on account of the enemy's drive still further to our right, and at about 2 o'clock I withdrew to form a flank along the Railway embankment from T.24.d.20.80 to the cross roads T.23.d.80. 40. and pushed men along the sunken road from this point to T.29.b.40.10. At this point I found that the ground held by me was too much for the number of men at my disposal, and had to withdraw men from the embankment T.25.d.20.80 to T.23.c.50.60 to strengthen the flank. Then I was joined by "B" Coy. under 2/Lt. Galsby, at the cross roads, who had come down along the SENSEE VALLEY from his stand to position in the Second System.

At this point I sent messages to Brigade Headquarters giving my position and stating that I was not sure of my flanks and also asking for assistance on the flanks. Whilst holding this position men gradually came back and I was further reinforced by one platoon from the 9th Bn., Northumberland Fus., and got touch between T.29.b.40.10 and T.29.c.55.70 - CIRCA. I sent one platoon to man Croiselles Switch at about T.23.a.50.30. I tried to man the high ground about T.29.d.25.40., but at each attempt the men sent forward became casualties and I had to abandon this project.

At this point an Officer of the Royal Scots brought information that Nelly Avenue was held as front line so again I rushed men out along the Railway embankment to link up. This attempt however was not successful owing to the length of the gap, and the number of men at my disposal. Again on account of pressure I found it necessary to reinforce my right flank. Parties of Royal Scots now came back from Croiselles along the road T.18.c.40.80 to T.23.d.00.65., who manned Croiselles Switch from T.23.d.40.10. to about T.23.a.70.80. I was in immediate touch with this garrison. With the reinforcements of the Brigade Pioneer Company, which now came up (at about 5 o'clock roughly) and which had orders to link up, I strengthened my right flank, between myself and the 9th Bn., Northumberland Fus. in the third system, as I was already in touch. I was then able to withdraw men from my right and man the trench between T.29.b.65.90. and T.23.d.40.20. This we held until ordered to withdraw at about 9 p.m.

When my first party was ready to move the enemy attempted to rush the S to rush the Sunken Road about T.23.b.35.40 to T.23.b.50.60 on the South-East. This was prevented by a rifle, Lewis Gun and Rifle Grenade fire, then by order I withdrew from this Sunken Road, commencing at about 6 o'clock, and held Croisselles Switch North from T.17.c.90.90 to T.17.b.50.10. This was completed by about 6-30am, the delay being caused by our finding this line occupied and held by the 103rd Brigade, who withdrew on relief by us. The garrison here was disposed 110 in the front line, one post of 10 being placed in the Sunken Road, about T.17.d.00.00. 70 men were in support in the Sunken Road T.17.c.30.45 to T.17.c.70.90. I established my H.Q. at about T.17.c.40.80. Between 3 and 4 a.m. a party of some 230 of the 23rd Bn., Northumberland Fus. joined us in the front line, and by order of the Officer commanding the Royal Scots, the Battalion on my left, were disposed 200 in the front line and 50 in support. Patrols were sent out in the village during the night, but could find no signs of enemy occupation.

At dawn the enemy recommenced his attack, massing behind the ridge along the 90 contour from point about T.17.d.70.00. running South-west, and as the morning was misty and visibility low found good cover. I reported this massing to Brigade H.Q. and arranged Artillery cooperation and assistance with Gunner Laison Officer. Little Artillery support however could be obtained. On our front the enemy attempted several attacks in small penetrating parties, but was beaten off by rifle and Lewis Gun fire. At about 8 a.m. the enemy broke through at T.23.a.60.55., and penetrated as far as the road junction T.23.a.20.65. I immediately organised a counter attack from the Sunken Road between T.17.a.25.50. to T.17.c.50.70., leading round into position from a line extending roughly from the cross roads T.17.c.65.50. to T.24.b.60.65. 2/Lt. Vipond with 2/Lts. Coleby and Bowmer were in charge of this counter attack. They gradually worked forward by sectional rushes, covered by Lewis and Vickers gun fire, and pressed the enemy right back. The success of this counter attack might have been very valuable, but at this point the enemy broke through on the left of the Royal Scots front, roughly between T.17.b.10.35 and T.17.a.80.70. Here the Royal Scots retired without warning, leaving my left flank in the air, and I was compelled to form a defensive flank over the Sunken Road from T.17.c.65.60 to about T.17.a.35.25., facing North-east. Under cover of this flank I withdrew with my garrison, but on account of the speed with which the enemy pressed his attack, and the difficulty of communication and the ground, a few of the more isolated parties of my line were cut off, fighting. I was 2/Lt. Peckston immediately before this withdrawal. On withdrawal (about 11 o'clock) I took up a position on Hill Switch on the right of the Royal Scots from T.16.b.20.20 and T.16.d.00.60. - CIRCA. After my line was organised and my posts in position, we were subjected to heavy enemy bombardment, and the line probably being broken on one of our left flank Battalions, the two Battalions on our left flank again withdrew without warning, in as it was impossible to obtain any information as to the reason for their retirement; and my left flank being exposed, I threw out a small cover flank under 2/Lt. Bowmer at about T.16.central, and successfully withdrew the remainder of my force to the third system firing line. On establishment here I reported in person to Brigade H.Q. I was then ordered to form a flank running back from T.16.central along 10.0 contour to about T.22.c.10.80 across to T.21.d.40.85 parallel with the road running North-west through T.21.b.& a. This was barely completed when the enemy broke through in front of St. Leger, and the order was given to withdraw and hold the third line firing system between T.21.c.35.35. and T.21.c.45.00.

At dusk much movement was seen on the enemy front, many various colored lights being sent up, and by the morning of the 23rd the enemy had pressed forward bringing up Pine Apple Trench Mortar to about T.22.c.50.55., and a Machine Gun to about T.21.b.55.55. As soon as daylight appeared, a great amount of enemy movement was seen about Hill Switch, and scouts and small bodies of men were seen advancing, and later continuous streams of men from about T.22.b.d. crossed the valley at T.15.central behind the Spur, at T.21.a, and 15.c. I again got in touch with the Artillery, and the advancing enemy were subjected to a heavy shell fire and fire from rifles and Lewis Guns. The

enemy casualties were seen to be heavy.     This attack did not materialise on our front, but seemed to strike further on our left.
At about 9 a.m. on the 23rd, our relief by troops of the 31st Division was begun, but in view of this attack by the enemy was not completed until about 3 p.m.
During the Relief there was no extensive enemy operation on our front.

---

DIARY of EVENTS of OPERATIONS from 4-30 a.m. to 1-30 p.m. March 21st 1918 by 2/Lt.OXTOBY A.H.of 25th Bn., Northumberland Fusiliers, being in reserve to the 102nd Brigade.

---

BATTALION HEADQUARTERS - BUNHILL ROW, U.25.d.

At 4-30 a.m., March 21st 1918, the enemy opened out with an intense bombardment, gas shells and H.E. shells being used. This bombardment continued until about 8-30 a.m., when there was a lull of about 20 minutes, followed by another bombardment which lasted until 11-30 a.m.

About this time reports reached Battalion H.Q. that the enemy had broken through on our right, but were held in check at VALLEY SUPPORT, U.21.c.3.2.

At 12 noon a message was received from Capt.Lavine 102nd T.M.B. to the effect that the enemy were in ECOUST, and he and 10 men were holding the ECOUST-CROISELLES Road.

At about 12-30 p.m. the Commanding Officer decided to move Battalion H.Q. to the H.Q. vacated by "A" Coy. at T.24.d.8.5. In consequence of this I received orders to move immediately. The Commanding Officer and Adjutant moved in advance, having decided to call at the H.Q. of the 22nd Northumberland Fusiliers. I last saw them close to the 22nd Northumberland Fusiliers H.Q. as I passed on my way to the new H.Q., where I arrived about 12-45 p.m., and waited for 30 minutes, but the C.O. and Adjutant did not reappear.

We then decided to return to Bunhill Row, but before this could be done the enemy were between us and the 22nd Northumberland Fusiliers H.Q., and we had to go back owing to heavy enemy Machine Gun and rifle fire.

We then reported to Capt. McLachlan at 1-30 p.m.

---

I am unable to furnish any further details than contained in the Diary compiled by Major McLachlan.

(Sgd)   A.H.OXTOBY, 2/Lt.

5/4/18.

34th Division.
102nd Infantry Brigade.

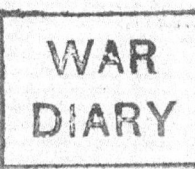

25th BATTALION

NORTHUMBERLAND FUSILIERS

APRIL 1 9 1 8

Army Form C. 2118.

# WAR DIARY
## or
## INTELLIGENCE SUMMARY

25th Bn Northumberland Fusiliers

April 1918

Vol 28

| Place | Date | Hour | Summary of Events and Information | Remarks and references to Appendices |
|---|---|---|---|---|
| ERQUINGHEM BRIGADE IN RESERVE | 1/4/18 to 4/4/18 | | The Battalion Paraded under Company arrangements from 9 am to 12.30 pm daily for Gas Drill, Lewis Gun Drill & Rifle Grenade Drill. Special time being allotted for reorganization. The subsidiar of the day the Companies were at the disposal of the 2nd i/c mark for refitting all ranks in the Battalion remained the front to the Division and the Brigade during this period. | |
| " | 5/4/18 | | The Battalion Paraded under Company arrangements from 9 am to 12.30 pm for Gas Drill Lewis Gun Drill & Rifle Grenade Drill. 1 hour was specially allotted for the reorganization of Companies. On the evening of the 6th about 8 pm the Battalion Relieved the 15th Bn Royal Scots in the front line trenches at HOUPLINES. Disposition "B" and "C" Companies in front line and "A" and "D" Companies in support occupying Billets in ARMENTIERS. Patrols were sent out by each of the Companies occupying the front line. During the night our Artillery was very active. | |
| HOUPLINES IN TRENCHES | 6/4/18 | | Enemy shelled communication trenches and subsidiary lines with 4.2" at intervals during the day and night. The back areas were shelled with 5.9's. Light Trench Mortar. Front line Posts and Communication trenches were active during the night on the | |
| " | 7/4/18 | | Enemy aircraft very active during the aft at 8 pm. The enemy bombarded ARMENTIERS with gas shells which continued until 6 am. On the following morning 8th April. Practically 60% of the Battalion were gassed including 13 in Hqrs | |

# WAR DIARY or INTELLIGENCE SUMMARY

Army Form C. 2118.

| Place | Date | Hour | Summary of Events and Information | Remarks and references to Appendices |
|---|---|---|---|---|
| HOUPLINES. IN TRENCHES. | 7/4/18 | | and The two Companies in Support. Machine Guns opened out occasional bursts of fire during the night. | |
| " | 8/4/18 | | Enemy aircraft again very active during the day. All seis craft were reported. About 7 p.m. The Battalion was reinforced by "C" Company of the 15th Royal Scots who took up position in the Subsidiary Line. Two platoons being allotted to each Company in the Front Line. At 11.20 p.m. a mine was blown up in front of any by R.E. which was intended as a Tank Trap. "B" Company provided two fighting patrols to prevent enemy from investigations. | |
| " | 9/4/18 | | Enemy aircraft again very active during the day. Very low flying. Major Allen took command of the Battalion. Enemy howitzer shelled our Communication Trenches but Subsidiary Line. Fighting Patrols sent out from each Company as usual at night. "C" Company 15th Royal Scots were withdrawn to Reserve. | |
| " | 10/4/18 | | Enemy low flying Aeroplanes were active on the whole of our Line throughout the day. Enemy attacked about many bombardments. The to bivouac on our left continued to shell our communication Trenches and | |

# WAR DIARY
## or
## INTELLIGENCE SUMMARY

Army Form C. 2118.

| Place | Date | Hour | Summary of Events and Information | Remarks and references to Appendices |
|---|---|---|---|---|
| HOUPLINES. IN TRENCHES. | 10/4/18 | | and Support Line. On account of enemy having penetrated the front on both flanks Houplines orders went receive about 3 p.m. for the withdrawal to the NORTH side of the RIVER L.Y.S. The withdrawal was carried out in an orderly manner without the enemy being aware of the movement. On reaching the River L.Y.S. we found that the bridge allotted to us was covered by enemy machine gun fire. Owing to this we moved along the river bank in an Easterly direction one half of the battalion crossing the river by the NIEPPE STONE BRIDGE and the other half crossing by pontoon bridges erected by the R.E's. "C" Company took posts on the NORTH bank of the river L.Y.S. on the EAST side of the ARMENTIER-NIEPPE Railway. "B" Company in support in NIEPPE SWITCH. Nothing of importance happened during the night. | |
| " | 11/4/18 | | at 7 am the Battalion was attacked in force but the enemy was repulsed by Rifle & machine gun fire. The attacked several times during the morning but gained no ground on the Battalion front. Owing to the enemy gaining ground on the flanks a position was taken up EAST of ARMENTIERS - NIEPPE Railway on the north of NIEPPE Railway at a more northern Right NIEPPE station and NIEPPE SWITCH. While in this position enemy was flying aeroplanes between | |

# WAR DIARY
or
## INTELLIGENCE SUMMARY
*(Erase heading not required.)*

Army Form C. 2118.

| Place | Date | Hour | Summary of Events and Information | Remarks and references to Appendices |
|---|---|---|---|---|
| IN THE TRENCHES. | 11/4/18 | | were very active. One enemy aeroplane was brought down by our airmen and one by Lifle machine gun fire. Both enemy machine fell on NORTH side of river LYS. The Battalion held its positions under continuous machine gun fire until orders were received at 7 p.m. for an orderly withdrawal to a prepared line NORTH of NIEPPE plank meeting on the NIEPPE BAILLEUL ROAD. This withdrawal was successfully carried out. The Brigade arrived near the Trenches before taking up positions. Men were fed and all had a few hours sleep. | |
| IN TRENCHES NORTH OF NIEPPE | 12/4/18 | | The Battalion took up positions in prepared line just NORTH of NIEPPE at 6 a.m. and remained in these positions during the day. Enemy two aeroplane flying very actively and occasionally opened fire from machine guns on our Trenches. This was replied to by our Lewis Guns. The Battalion remained in this position during the day. Patrols were sent out to keep in touch with the Battalion in the front line. | |
| " | 13/4/18 | | On the morning of the 13th the enemy attacked the Battalion on my left firing Stokes trench mortars answered by the following by Rifle and Lewis Machine Gun fire. At about 8 p.m. the enemy | |

# WAR DIARY or INTELLIGENCE SUMMARY

Army Form C. 2118.

| Place | Date | Hour | Summary of Events and Information | Remarks and references to Appendices |
|---|---|---|---|---|
| IN TRENCHES NOR.TH. OF NIEPPE | 13/4/18 | | and drove a heavy counterattack on the left Battalion front. "C" Company 25th to 19th North'd Fus was sent to reinforce the left Battalion. At about 5 p.m. the remaining Company reinforced the next Battalion also filled a gap between our own Division (34th) and the Division on our left. At 7 p.m. the enemy forced the troops both right & left. Heavy machine firing Rifle fire was brought to bear on him by our Division. 2/Lt Grieveby was now in command of the Battalion 2/Lt Jacoby was now in command of the Battalion 2/Lt ? Company. Owing to heavy casualties The Brigade was re-arranged as a Battalion. The 21st Battalion forming one Company. Positions were held until orders for withdrawal were issued. | |
| " | 14/4/18 | | At 2 a.m. orders were received to withdraw through lines occupied by fresh troops. The Battalion Company assembled at a Farm just East of LA Creche & were moved to Billets about 1 Kilometre EAST of BAILEUL. At 3 p.m. the Battalion Company received orders to assemble at the main junction of the Mt NOIR – BAILEUL ROAD. The Battalion Company was organised into 4 Platoons. The Brigade (? Battalion) was commanded by Lt Col ? A.S.C. | |

Army Form C. 2118.

# WAR DIARY
## or
## INTELLIGENCE SUMMARY
(Erase heading not required.)

Instructions regarding War Diaries and Intelligence Summaries are contained in F. S. Regs., Part II. and the Staff Manual respectively. Title pages will be prepared in manuscript.

| Place | Date | Hour | Summary of Events and Information | Remarks and references to Appendices |
|---|---|---|---|---|
| IN TRENCHES. NORTH of NIEPPE | 14/4/18 | | 2nd Lt Colder took lt[?]/[?]fours of the Battalion forward and eighteen new positions. These positions were reconnoitred and the Company was then alerted. The men dug themselves in and remained in all night. | |
| IN TRENCHES NORTH OF BAILLEUL | 15/4/18 | | Nothing of importance happened during the morning. The Battalion Company was ordered to march at 2 p.m. to HOGINACKER CAMP and remained here a few hours. At about 5 p.m. the enemy heavily bombarded the Front line at the same time shelled the Camp. The Camp was cleared and a position taken up in trenches just EAST of the CAMP at 7 p.m. orders were received to take up a position in Trenches in rear of an Battalion at junction of Mt. NOIR — BAILLEUL ROAD. Dispositions. Two platoons in front line and Two Platoons in Support. Enemy aircraft very active during the day. | |
| " | 16/4/18 | | The Battalion Company at 9 a.m. became [?] line [?] advancing [?] Division to withdraw through it. Enemy shelled positions heavily throughout the day and his aircraft was very active reconnaissance [?]. Machine gun into new trenches which suffered very few casualties from Rifle Fire. All work shown the greatest coolness courage under these trying circumstances | |

# WAR DIARY or INTELLIGENCE SUMMARY

*(Erase heading not required.)*

| Place | Date | Hour | Summary of Events and Information | Remarks and references to Appendices |
|---|---|---|---|---|
| IN TRENCHES NORTH OF BAILLEUL. | 17/4/18 | | Enemy artillery and own Aircraft very active throughout the day. Enemy attacked the Battalion on our right just after dark with a mixture of H.E. and Gas. No infantry action followed. Enemy shelled our positions intermittently throughout the day with a mixture of H.E. and Gas. Patrols were sent out about 10pm from Front Line Posts and reported enemy in RAILWAY SIDING about 400 yds SOUTH EAST of the junction of the MT.NOIR – BAILLEUL ROADS. The remainder of the night was quiet. | |
| " | 18/4/18 | | Enemy barrage commenced the previous own evening followed. Enemy shelled our positions intermittently throughout the day with Enemy's low flying Planes again very active. Patrols were sent out from Front Line Posts. 3 Prisoners were brought in by the Battalion on our left. Nothing of importance happened during the night. | |
| " | 19/4/18 | | On the morning of the 19th our Artillery shelled BAILLEUL with gas shells. Enemy aircraft was active during the day and was heavily engaged by our Anti-Aircraft Guns. Remainder of the day was quiet. Patrols were sent out as usual but did not come in contact with the enemy. Situation throughout the night was normal. | |
| " | 20/4/18 | | Enemy frequently bombarded Battalion on our left – again with infantry action followed through. Artillery on both sides was very active during the day and also Enemy Rifle accurate on the afternoon that the Battalion would be relieved by 6th Sussex shelled our Front and Support & Front line in and such a ruse at dusk. |

Army Form C. 2118.

# WAR DIARY
## or
## INTELLIGENCE SUMMARY  25th Battn: Northumberland Fusiliers

(Erase heading not required.)

Instructions regarding War Diaries and Intelligence Summaries are contained in F. S. Regs., Part II. and the Staff Manual respectively. Title pages will be prepared in manuscript.

| Place | Date | Hour | Summary of Events and Information | Remarks and references to Appendices |
|---|---|---|---|---|
| CROIX-du- POPERINGHE | 21/4/18 | 2. am | The Battalion was relieved by the French, the relief being complete by 2. am. The Battalion marched via BOESCHEPPE K.L. 33.C.8.8. | |
| | 22/4/18 | | The Battalion turned out at 10.30 am and marched via WATOU to SAN-JANS-TER-BIEZEN Camp. | |
| SAN-JANS- -TER-BIEZEN | 23/4/18 | | The Battalion paraded at the disposal of O/C Companies for re-organisation. | |
| " | 24/4/18 | | The Battalion paraded. Physical Training, Lewis Gunners and Signallers with their own instructors. Remainder of day devoted to re-organisation. | |
| " | 25/4/18 | | The Battalion provided a working & all available men and were engaged upon the improvement of the R.E. dump constructing the POPERINGHE ARMY LINE. | |
| " | 26/4/18 | | The Brigade received orders to occupy the POPERINGHE ARMY LINE. The Battalion turned out at 8.30 am and marched through SAN-JANS-ter-BIEZEN village via Swish Road N.W.65 POPERINGHE to its position. On the evening of the 26th the Battalion received further orders to move South and occupy the Southern Sector of the POPERINGHE ARMY LINE. Two officers & one Company reconnoitred the BRANDHOEK HOOP LINE. | |

Army Form C. 2118.

# WAR DIARY
## or
## INTELLIGENCE SUMMARY. 25th Bn Northumberland Fusiliers

(Erase heading not required.)

Instructions regarding War Diaries and Intelligence Summaries are contained in F.S. Regs., Part II. and the Staff Manual respectively. Title pages will be prepared in manuscript. April 1918.

| Place | Date | Hour | Summary of Events and Information | Remarks and references to Appendices |
|---|---|---|---|---|
| POPERINGHE ARMY LINE | 27/4/18 | | Brigade received orders to hold the BRANDHOEK HOOPLINE. The Battalion being kept in reserve and in case of hostile attack to hold the POPERINGHE ARMY LINE from the POPERINGHE–YPRES ROAD to the POPERINGHE–RENINGHELST ROAD. Dispositions A Company on the right "D" Company on the left, "C" Company on the Centre "B" Company in support. | |
| " | 28/4/18 | | The Battalion provided working parties of 249 men and continued the work on the POPERINGHE System under the supervision of the R.E.'s | |
| " | 29/4/18 | | The Battalion provided working parties of 100 men and continued the work on the POPERINGHE System. | |
| " | 30/4/18 | | The Battalion provided working parties of 247 men and continued working on the POPERINGHE System. | |

P.L. Lincoln Major
Commanding 25th Bn Northumberland Fus.

102nd Brigade.
34th Division.

25th NORTHUMBELAND FUSILIERS

M A Y   1 9 1 8.

Army Form C. 2118.

# WAR DIARY

## INTELLIGENCE SUMMARY.

25th Bn Northumberland Fusiliers

May 1918

(Erase heading not required.)

Instructions regarding War Diaries and Intelligence Summaries are contained in F. S. Regs., Part II. and the Staff Manual respectively. Title pages will be prepared in manuscript.

| Place | Date | Hour | Summary of Events and Information | Remarks and references to Appendices |
|---|---|---|---|---|
| POPERINGHE ARMY LINE Left Subsector | 1/5/18 | | Battn provided working parties of 390 men and carried out the construction of a new support line, improving & completing of outposts & trenches under the supervision of O/c 208 Field Coy. R.E.'s in the POPERINGHE System. | |
| | 2/5/18 | | Battn supplied 446 men as working parties and was employed for 8 hrs under the O/c 208 Field Coy. R.E.'s digging new support line, mining & completing Strong Posts & Trenches | |
| " | 3/5/18 | | Battn furnished 353 men as working parties and was employed on the POPERINGHE System under the O/c 208 Field Coy. R.E.'s digging Support Lines, Winning & placing Forward Trenches in a state of defence. | |
| " | 4/5/18 | | Battn furnished 332 men as working parties under the O/c 208 Field Coy. R.E.'s and was employed on the POPERINGHE System, digging Support Trenches, Winning Outposts and Camouflaging Trenches. | |
| " | 5/5/18 | | Battn provided 355 men as working parties and continued work in progress in the POPERINGHE System from 8.30 a.m. to 12.30 p.m. The Battalion was relieved by the 9th Bn Northumberland Fusiliers about 6 p.m. On relief Coys mvd marched independently to their Camps at L.7.4.1.9. All moves being made by parties not greater than Platoons at 200 yds interval. | |
| L.7.4.1.9. 1 Mile East of Sans-jans-bq BIEZEN | 6/5/18 | | The Battalion furnished at the disposal of O/c Companies for cleaning up | |

A5834 Wt. W4973/M687 750,000 8/16 D.D.&I. Ltd. Forms/C.2118/13.

# WAR DIARY / INTELLIGENCE SUMMARY

**Army Form C. 2118.**

Instructions regarding War Diaries and Intelligence Summaries are contained in F.S. Regs., Part II. and the Staff Manual respectively. Title pages will be prepared in manuscript.

(Erase heading not required.)

| Place | Date | Hour | Summary of Events and Information | Remarks and references to Appendices |
|---|---|---|---|---|
| L.7.4.1.9. EAST of SANJAN-SI-BIEZEN | 7/5/18 | | The Battalion paraded at the disposal of Coy. Commanders for training. Lewis gunners & Signallers paraded with their own Specialists. 1 Officer & 4 men per Company attended Brigade Lewis Gun Course. 1 N.C.O. per Platoon attended Brigade Musketry course. | |
| " | 8/5/18 | | The Battalion paraded 9 a.m. to 12.30 p.m. under Coy. Commanders for manual, squad and platoon drill. Specialists, Lewis gunners & Signallers with their own Instructors. Battalion paraded at 10 a.m. in battle order in front of Coy Tents under General Thwaites, instructor Musketry under Southern Army. General Thwaites inspected N.C.O's linen. The following N.C.O's passed:– <br> 47048 Sgt. W.H. Ryan <br> 47066 L/Cpl. R. Turner <br> 6890 Pte. H. Collins <br> 46998 Pte. T. Wren <br> 47033 Pte. W.J. Perry | |
| " | 9/5/18 | | The Battalion paraded 9 a.m. to 12 a.m. at disposal of Coy. Commanders. Specialists, Lewis gunners & Signallers under their own Instructors. At 12.15. Memorial Service for all Denominations except R.C. | |
| " | 10/5/18 | | The Battalion Paraded. 9 a.m. to 1 p.m. at disposal of Coy. Commanders for Lewis Gun Drill, Musketry & Coy Open Order Drill. Officers Course under Brigade Musketry Instructor. | |

# WAR DIARY
## or
## INTELLIGENCE SUMMARY
*(Erase heading not required.)*

Army Form C. 2118.

Instructions regarding War Diaries and Intelligence Summaries are contained in F. S. Regs., Part II. and the Staff Manual respectively. Title pages will be prepared in manuscript.

| Place | Date | Hour | Summary of Events and Information | Remarks and references to Appendices |
|---|---|---|---|---|
| L.T.M.G. 1 MILE EAST OF | 11/5/18 | | The Battalion Parade 9am to 1pm at disposal of Company Commanders for Lewis Gun Drill Musketry & Platoon Drills. Remainder of afternoon spent in refitting men. | — |
| SAN JANS-TER BIEZEN | | | | |
| " | 12/5/18 | | The Battalion paraded at 7.30am and marched through WATOU — HOUTKERQUE — HERZELLE — WORMHOUDT to RUBROUCK. | — |
| RUBROUCK | 13/5/18 | | The Battalion paraded at 6.20am on the main LEDERZEELE-ZEGGERS CAPPEL ROAD and marched to rail junction in HERKELSBRUGGE where they entrained by Bus to LOTTINGHEM and from there marched to VERVAL. | — |
| VERVAL | 14/5/18 | | The Battalion paraded at eighteen of Company Commanders for cleaning up etc. | — |
| " | 15/5/18 | | The Battalion was formed into a Battalion Training Cadre. Instructors paraded under 8th Corps Instructors in Lewis Gun, Musketry etc. Surplus paraded under Company Commanders for training. Parades 9am to 1/5pm | — |
| " | 16/5/18 | | | — |
| " | 17/5/18 | | Surplus personnel of Battalion paraded at 5.45am & proceeded by march to DESVRES when they entrained for the Base at 10-10am. Instructional Staff continued training under 8th Corps Instructors in Lewis Gun Musketry etc | — |

# WAR DIARY
## INTELLIGENCE SUMMARY

Army Form C. 2118.

| Place | Date | Hour | Summary of Events and Information | Remarks and references to Appendices |
|---|---|---|---|---|
| VERVAL | 18/5/18 | | Battalion Training Cadre paraded at 1pm & marched to the BLEQUIN Sub Area at Headquarters, "C"Cy & Transport to LA CALIQUE. "A"Cy BLEQUIN, "B"Cy SENLECQUES & "D"Cy to LOTTINGHEM. Arrangements were then made to billet Battalion & the 110th U.S.A. Regt. | |
| LA CALIQUE | 19/5/18 | | Continued billeting Arrangements for U.S.A. Troops. Instructor continued training in all subjects in preparation for American Troops. Capt J. Oley + 2/Lt J.S. Bowmer received Billeting Areas | |
| | 20/5/18 | | 1st & 3rd Batts of 110th U.S.A. arrived & billets at BLEQUIN & LOTTINGHEM at 11am. Regt | |
| " | 21/5/18 | | 110th US Regt Headquarters arrived in billets at LA CALIQUE at 11.15 m. | |
| " | 22/5/18 | | 2nd Batt 110 US Regt arrived in billets at SENLECQUES at 12 midnight. | |
| " | 23/5/18 | | Pending orders for Training American Units, instruction & lectures were given to Officers & NCO's of 110th U.S. Regt | |
| " | 24/5/18 | | "A"Cy BLEQUIN. Arrangements made & start Training 1st Batt U.S.A. 110th Regt on Bomb. 27/5/18, permission for assault course & 30 yd Range. Instructors being sent to this Cy. | |
| | | 8.70 a.m 11-12 a.m 2-30 pm-4.30 pm | "B"Cy SENLECQUES. Instruction given to 2nd Batt 110th Regt U.S.A in Musketry, Gas, Lewis Gun. Lectures to each Cy in turn by Capt Coleby on "Duties & responsibilities of NCOs & Junior Service | |
| | | 9-30 a.m 12 - noon 2-30 p.m - 4.30 p.m | "D"Cy LOTTINGHEN. Instructor given to I Cy. 3rd Bn H. 110th Regt U.S.A. in Musketry K Cy. | |

# WAR DIARY
## OF
## INTELLIGENCE SUMMARY.
*(Erase heading not required.)*

Army Form C. 2118.

Instructions regarding War Diaries and Intelligence Summaries are contained in F. S. Regs., Part II. and the Staff Manual respectively. Title pages will be prepared in manuscript.

| Place | Date | Hour | Summary of Events and Information | Remarks and references to Appendices |
|---|---|---|---|---|
| LA CALIQUE | 24/5/18 | 9-20am to 11-30am | Headquarters LACALIQUE. Instructors given to Hdqrs Co, 110th Regt U.S.A. in Musketry | |
| " | 25/5/18 | 9-30am to 11-30am | "A" Co BLEQUIN, Instructors with 1st Batt 110th Regt in Musketry Lewis gun. | |
| | | | LOTTINGHEM | |
| | | | "B" Co FIENVILLERS, Instructors with "M" Co 3rd Batt in morning + "L" Co in afternoon. | |
| | | 2pm | "B" Co SENLECQUES. Morning). Instructors with 2nd Batt in Musketry Lewis Gun Gas | |
| | | 4pm | Afternoon). Route march men Field Kitchens on line of march. | |
| | 26/5/18 | | Voluntary C of E + R.C. Services. Open to all Troops | |
| | | 4-30pm | Meeting of OC 110th USA Regt + Batt Commanders with OC 25th North'd Fus + Co Commanders to arrange Training of American Regt to start 27/5/18 | |
| | 27/5/18 | 8-30am to 11-30am | American Divisional Training Schedule started British Instructors attached | |
| | " | 12-30pm to 3-30pm | 3rd Batt 110th Regt U.S.A. fired on ESCOEVILLES Range | |
| | | | | |
| | | | 1st do | |
| | 28/5/18 | | | |
| | 29/5/18 | | | |
| | 30/5/18 | | American Holiday (Decoration Day) Commander in Chief U.S.A. Army visited the Division | |
| | 31/5/18 | | Training as per Schedule continued | |

Lt Lincoln Lintott
Lt Lincoln Lintott
Comdg 25th N.F.

A5834 Wt. W4973/M687 750,000 8/16 D. D. & L. Ltd. Forms/C.2118/13.

102nd Brigade.
34th Division.

Battalion transferred to
39th Division 17.6.18.

25th NORTHUMBERLAND FUSILIERS

JUNE 1918

# WAR DIARY
## or
## INTELLIGENCE SUMMARY.

*(Erase heading not required.)*

Army Form C. 2118.

25th North'n Fus.

| Place | Date | Hour | Summary of Events and Information | Remarks and references to Appendices |
|---|---|---|---|---|
| LA CALIQUE | 1/6/18 | 5-30am to 11-30am 12-30pm to 3-30pm | End of first weeks training of 110th USA Regt as per Schedule. | |
| " | 2/6/18 | | 110th American Regt held Mass Parade followed by Church Service | |
| " | 3/6/18 to 7/6/18 | 6-30am to 11-30am 12-30pm to 2-30pm | British Instructors assist in second weeks training of 110th USA Regt as per Schedule | |
| " | 8/6/18 | | American Troops hand in British rifles, bayonets + Gas American Arms before marching away | |
| " | 9/6/18 | 12-30pm | 110th Regt. 28th American Div. marched away on three days march before entraining | |
| " | 10/6/18 | | Coy HdQrs. marched into LA CALIQUE | |
| LE WAST | 11/6/18 | | 25th North'n Fus Batt. Training Cadre marched to LE WAST to billet 309th M.G. Batt. and 311th + 312th MG Coys. 78th American Division. | |
| " | 12/6/18 | | 311th + 312th American MG Coys arrived in Billets | |
| " | 13/6/18 | | | |
| " | 14/6/18 15/6/18 | | M.G. Coys started training; under plan drawn arrangement with assistance of British Instructor. Evening Lecture given by C.I.O. + Lecture on "Food + Rations in Active Service" by O. i/c Inf. |  |
| " | 16/6/18 | | Church Parades. | |

Army Form C. 2118.

# WAR DIARY
## *or*
## INTELLIGENCE SUMMARY.

(Erase heading not required.)

25th North'd Fus.

| Place | Date | Hour | Summary of Events and Information | Remarks and references to Appendices |
|---|---|---|---|---|
| LE WAST | 19/4/18 to 28/4/18 | | M.G. Units carried out first fortnight Training of 78th American Division programme. British Instructors assisting. Schools in Gas, Bombing & Musketry under British Instructors have been in progress. | |
| | 29/4/18 | | | |
| | 30/4/18 | | 25th North'd Fus Batt. Training Cadre marched to ALQUINES to meet the Training of 309th American Infy Regt | |

J.L. Ewbank Lieut Col.
Comdg 25th North'd Fus.

Army Form C. 2118.

# WAR DIARY
## or
## INTELLIGENCE SUMMARY.
*(Erase heading not required.)*

VR 31

| Place | Date | Hour | Summary of Events and Information | Remarks and references to Appendices |
|---|---|---|---|---|
| ALQUINES | July 1st to 17th | | Assisted in the training of 309th American Regt as per weekly Schedule attached. All units fired a course on both long & short range also a course of Bombing. Grist aspirants are given a short training by 39th Divn Demonstration Platoon. | |
| | 18th | | 309th American Regt with 227th Brit’sd moved by motor & rail to CHELERS | |
| CHELERS | 19th to 31st | | Training of 309th American Regt continued as per Schedule | |

H. Lincoln Lieut Col
Comdg 25th North’d Fus

309th Infantry,
A.E.F., France, June 29, 1918.

## SCHEDULE FOR WEEK JULY 1 TO JULY 6.

|  |  |
|---|---|
| 8:30 to 9:30 | Battalion Commanders (See *) |
| 9:30 to 10:30 | Outpost, Patrolling, Advance, Rear & Flank Guard, Deployment of Platoons & Companies for attack and defensive. Training Memo. Hdqrs 78th Div.(d) |
| 10:30 to 11:00 | Gas |
| 11:00 to 11:30 | Close Order, Companies & Platoons. |
| 11:30 to 12:30 | Dinner |
| 12:30 to 1:00 | New Platoon Formation (Supplement to the Offensive Conduct of Small Units, Pamphlet 160-A) |
| 1:00 to 2:00 | Musketry. Instruction in the use of Infantry Weapons. |
| 2:00 to 2:30 | Close Order, Company and Platoon. |

1. Hours of work on training ground will be from 8:30 a.m. to 2:30 p.m., with an interval for dinner (haversack rations) from 11:30 to 12:30 p.m.

2. Light packs and respirators will be carried on all drills. Gas masks to be used from time to time in all drills, total of at least 1 hour per day. Helmets to be worn at least 2 hours per day or may be worn exclusively.

3. Bayonet fighting as per preceding week.

4. Ranges will be kept in use by Battalions at all times.

*5. It is suggested that the 1st half hour of the period be devoted to games and athletics to liven the men up. The other half hour to Battalion in attack and defense.

6. A class of 20 men per company will be trained in Lewis Gun (N.C.O. and selected Privates). The instruction will be conducted by our own instructors and the remaining British Instructors.
These men will be assembled in groups of 8 men and will form part of the same group during the week. Senior men in each group will carry a list of names of men in group and name of instructor. In each Battalion these groups will be arranged as follows : 1 Company, 2 groups of 8, the remaining 4 to be consolidated with the other remaining 4 of the next Company. Groups and instructors will assemble in NE end of 2nd Battalion drill ground. Each company will send out a Lewis Gun for each group of 8, except that the first and third companies in the Battalion will send one additional gun to be used in the consolidation of the extra 4 men from each company.

7. Gas demonstration at Harlettes Gas Ground, prescribed in Training Memo #8 will be held as follows:
        1st Battalion, July 1
        2nd Battalion, July 2
        3rd Battalion, July 3
First Company in each Battalion will report at 9:30 a.m., 2nd at 10:30, 3rd at 11:30 and fourth at 12:30. All men in each Company will attend including those attending regimental school.

8. Regimental or Battalion Practice march as prescribed in (c) Training memo #5, will be held Friday, July 5th. Instructions as to time and assumed situation will be announced later.

BY ORDER OF COLONEL MORGAN:

R.A.SEGARRA
Capt & Adjt 309th Infantry,
Adjutant.

309th Infantry
A.E.F. France, July 5, 18.

## SCHEDULE FOR WEEK JULY 8 TO JULY 13.

| | |
|---|---|
| 8:30 to 10:00 | Company and Platoon Commanders (New Platoon) (See *) |
| 10:00 to 11:00 | Outpost, Patrolling Advance, Rear & Flank Guard, Deployment of Platoons & Companies for attack and defense. Training Memo. Hdqrs. 78th Div. (d) |
| 11:00 to 11:30 | Close Order, Companies and Platoons. |
| 11:30 to 12:30 | Dinner. |
| 12:30 to 1:00 | New Platoon Formation (Supplement to the Offensive Conduct of Small Units, Pamphlet 160-A) |
| 1:00 to 2:00 | Battalion as outpost, Advance Guard, Rear Guard, Flank Guard, Deployment for attack and defense. Training Memo. Hdqrs. 78th Div. (d) |
| 2:00 to 2:30 | Close Order, Company and Platoon |

1. Hours of work on training ground will be from 8:30 a.m. to 2:30 p.m., with an interval for dinner (haversack rations) from 11:30 to 12:30 p.m.

2. Light packs and respirators will be carried on all drills. Gas masks to be used from time to time in all drills, total of at least 1 hour per day. Helmets to be worn at least 2 hours per day or may be worn exclusively.

3. Bayonet fighting as per preceding week.

4. Ranges will be kept in use by Battalions at all times.

*5. It is suggested that the 1st half hour of the period be devoted to games and athletics to liven the men up. The other hour to Company and Platoon in attack and defense.

6. The same class of 20 men per company will be trained in Lewis Gun (N.C.O. and selected Privates). The instruction will be conducted by our own instructors and the remaining British Instructors.
These men will be assembled in groups of 8 men and will form part of the same group during the week. Senior men in each group will carry a list of names of men in group and name of instructor. In each Battalion these groups will be arranged as follows: 1 Company, 2 groups of 8, the remaining 4 to be consolidated with the other remaining 4 of the next Company. Groups and instructors will assemble in NE end of 2nd Battalion drill ground. Each company will send out a Lewis Gun for each group of 8, except that the first and third companies in the Battalion will send one additional gun to be used in the consolidation of the extra 4 men from each company.

7. Gas demonstration at Harlettes Gas Ground, prescribed in Training Memo #8 will be held as follows:
        1st Battalion, July 11
        2nd Battalion, July 12
First Company in each Battalion will report at 9:30 a.m. 2nd at 10:30, 3rd at 11:30 and fourth at 12:30. All men in each company will attend including those attending regimental school

8. Regimental march as prescribed in (c) Training Memo #5, will be held Friday, July 12th. Instructions as to time and assumed situation will be announced later.

9. Especial attention to march discipline in march to and from drill grounds. Battalion, Company and Platoon Commanders will march in rear of their units from time to time and check any breeches of march discipline.

                          BY ORDER OF COLONEL MORGAN:
                              EDWARD D. ARNOLD,
                      Capt. & Adjt. 309th Infantry,
                            Acting Adjutant.

309th Infantry,
A.E.F., France,
13 July 1918.

## SCHEDULE FOR WEEK JULY 15 TO JULY 20

8:30 to 11:30 a.m.   Tactical exercises by Company & Battalion.*
12:30 to  2:30 p.m.  Bayonet, Target Practice 30 yd range, Close
                     Order, Bombing, Lewis Gun.

    1.   Dates and hours of target practice (long range) special demonstrations etc., will be announced from time to time.

    2.   Lewis guns will be taken on all tactical exercises.

    3.   Battalion Commanders will assume a tactical situation, and special attention will be paid to the handling of Lewis Guns, and liaison.

    4.   Light packs and respirators will be carried on all drills. Gas masks to be used from time to time in all drills, total of at least 1 hour per day.  Helmets to be worn at least 2 hours per day or may be worn exclusively.

    5.   *It is suggested that the first half hour of the afternoon period be devoted to games and athletics to liven the men up.

    6.   Gas demonstration at Harlettes Gas Ground for 2nd Battalion will be held Monday, July 15th, 1918, as follows:

              1st Co.  9:30 a.m.
              2nd Co. 10:30 a.m.
              3rd Co. 11:30 a.m.
              4th Co. 12:30 p.m.


BY ORDER OF COLONEL MORGAN,


R.A. SEGARRA,
Capt. & Adjt., 309th Infantry,
Adjutant.

Headquarters, 309th Infantry,
A.E.F., France, July 20th, 1918.

Memorandum:-

1. Until further orders, the following Training Program will be followed by Battalion and Headquarters Commanders at their respective stations. Training periods from 8:30 a.m. to 11:30 a.m. and from 1:00 p.m. to 3:00 p.m.

```
8:30  to  9:00 - Inspection of arms and equipment (daily)
9:00  to  9:30 - Games and athletics.
9:30  to 10:30 - Close Order drill - Company and Platoon
10:30 to 11:00 - Manual of Arms
11:00 to 11:30 - Anti-gas Instruction
1:00  to  3:00 - Instruction in Platoon Leadership
```

2. In the period devoted to Close Order drill and manual of arms, strict attention will be paid to discipline and smartness in movements.

3. Platoon Commanders will personally make the inspection of arms and equipment during the time allotted and will see that arms and equipment are properly cared for. Company Commanders will superintend this inspection.

4. In the afternoon period instructions in Platoon Leadership, Platoon Commanders and Squad Leaders will be given the opportunity to become thoroughly acquainted with every man in his unit and all enlisted men encouraged and instructed in taking command of larger units in emergency. Special stress to be paid to this subject. At the same time men should be instructed in the squad, platoon, company, battalion and regimental organization.

5. During the one-half hour period assigned to anti-gas instruction, special attention will be given to the subject of gas shells, their recognition and the necessary drill in securing quick protection and spreading the alarm. In addition Battalion Commanders will designate one day in the week when all officers and men will wear their masks for a continuous period of one hour, and this time to be duly recorded in each case.

6. Regimental Commander directs that Company and Platoon Commanders make special effort to organize new Lewis Gunners, and each platoon commander keep his gun teams at the highest pitch of efficiency.

7. In case no suitable ground for drilling is available, the roads near by will be used, care being taken not to obstruct traffic.

8. Battalion Adjutants will report at Regimental Headquarters daily at 4:00 p.m. to receive necessary orders and instructions. Supply and Headquarters Company will send representatives.

9. Battalion and Company Commanders will report at Regimental Headquarters on Sundays at 11:00 a.m.

BY ORDER OF COLONEL MORGAN:

R. A. SEGARRA
Capt. & Adjt. 309th Infantry,
Adjutant.

CONFIDENTIAL

# WAR DIARY

of

25th Batn Northumb Fus.

From Aug 1st 1918
To    "   31st  "

Vol No _____

Army Form C. 2118.

Maps {LENS 11, CALAIS 13, DIEPPE 16}

# WAR DIARY
## or
## INTELLIGENCE SUMMARY.

(Erase heading not required.)

25th North'd Fus.

Instructions regarding War Diaries and Intelligence Summaries are contained in F. S. Regs., Part II. and the Staff Manual respectively. Title pages will be prepared in manuscript.

| Place | Date | Hour | Summary of Events and Information | Remarks and references to Appendices |
|---|---|---|---|---|
| CHELERS | 1/5/15 to 3/5/15 | | Training of 78th American Division under British completed. | |
| | 4/5/15 | | Cadre Batt. moves by road & rail to LICQUES Area | |
| LICQUES | 5/5/15 to 14/5/15 | | Parades in morning. Recreation in afternoon. | |
| | 15/5/15 | | Moved by road & rail to ABANCOURT Area, Infantry Camp | |
| ABANCOURT | 23/5/15 | | Moved by road to Haudricourt Camp | |
| HAUDRICOURT | 24/5/15 to 31/5/15 | | Preparing Camp & making arrangements for reception of Reinforcements | |

J.L. Lincoln Lieut Col
Commdg 25th North'd Fus.

CONFIDENTIAL

WAR DIARY

OF

25th Bn. NORTHUMBERLAND FUSILIERS.

From 1st. September 1918.   to   30th. September 1918.

Army Form C. 2118.

# WAR DIARY
## or
## INTELLIGENCE SUMMARY.
(Erase heading not required)

| Place | Date | Hour | Summary of Events and Information | Remarks and references to Appendices |
|---|---|---|---|---|
| HAUDRICOURT | 1/9/18. | | 1st to 30th. Preparing No. 1. I of C Area Reception Camp for arrival of Malarial Reinforcements. | |
| " | 2/9/18. | | Lieut-Colonel P.L. Lincoln proceeded to United Kingdom on Special Leave. Captain F.L. Allan temporary command of the Battalion. | |
| " | 17/9/18. | | Lieut-Colonel. P.L. Lincoln resumed command of Battalion on return from leave. | |
| " | 18/9/18. | | Personnel 192 O.R. Malarial Reinforcements of the Cheshire Regiment, East Lancashire and Manchester Regiments arrived. | |
| " | 24/9/18. | | Personnel of the Manchester Regiment were cross-posted to 23rd. Bn. Northumberland Fusiliers. | |
| " | 25/9/18. | | Personnel Malarial Reinforcements of Kings Own Royal Lancasters arrived. G.O.C. L. of C. Area visited Camp. | |
| " | 28/9/18. | | Malarial Reinforcements of Munsters, Royal Dublin, Royal Irish and Inniskilling Fusiliers arrived. | |
| " | 30/9/18. | | Personnel Malarial Reinforcements, Royal Irish, Munsters, Leinster and Dublin Fusiliers arrived. | |

Major
Commanding 25th Bn. Northd. Fusiliers.

CONFIDENTIAL.
-------------

WAR DIARY.

of

25TH BN. NORTHUMBERLAND FUSILIERS.
-------------

From 1ST. OCTOBER, 1918.     To 31st. OCTOBER, 1918.

Army Form C. 2118.

# WAR DIARY
## or
## INTELLIGENCE SUMMARY.
*(Erase heading not required.)*

Instructions regarding War Diaries and Intelligence Summaries are contained in F. S. Regs., Part II. and the Staff Manual respectively. Title pages will be prepared in manuscript.

Vol 34

| Place | Date | Hour | Summary of Events and Information | Remarks and references to Appendices |
|---|---|---|---|---|
| HAUDRICOURT | 1/9/18 | | 1st to 31st Administrating & training Malarial Reinforcements as previous month. | |
| | 2/9/18 | | LT. COL. P.L. LINCOLN PROCEEDED to ITALY to join 10th NORTHUM'D FUS MAJOR. M. CATCHPOLE IN COMMAND OF BATTAL'. | p.16 |
| | 5/9/18 | | CAPTAIN & ADJ'T H.S. HOBSON Proceeded to join 7th NORFOLK REG'T 2nd Lt BOUMER appointed a/Adjt | p.18 |
| | 24/9/18 | | 251 O.Rs. despatched as reinforcements to line. | p.13 |
| | | | 160. OR'S Total reinforcements received for month. | p.15 |

M.C. Catchpole

CONFIDENTIAL.

# WAR DIARY

## OF

### 25TH. BN. NORTHUMBERLAND FUSILIERS.

From :- 1st. Novr, 1918.  TO :- 30th NOVR. 1918.

****************************

( COLUME XXI ).

# WAR DIARY
## or
## INTELLIGENCE SUMMARY.

Army Form C. 2118.

| Place | Date | Hour | Summary of Events and Information | Remarks and references to Appendices |
|---|---|---|---|---|
| HAUDRICOURT | 1/5/145 | | 1st to 30th administration, training medical reinforcements as previous month. | |
| " | 9th | | Major B intituled join the Batt. | 9.5.15 |
| " | 25th | | 57 Reinforcements despatched to front. | 25.5.15 |
| " | 30th | | 119 Reinforcements despatched to front. Total Reinforcements received for month 1014. | 25.5.15 |

A.A. Balckpole Lt Colonel
Commanding 25th Yorkshire Lancs
Regt.

TRAINING CADRE
39TH DIVISION
DIVL TROOPS

25TH BN NORTH'D FUS.
JAN - APR 1919

66 DIV

## WAR DIARY
or
## INTELLIGENCE SUMMARY.

Army Form C. 2118.

| Place | Date | Hour | Summary of Events and Information | Remarks and references to Appendices |
|---|---|---|---|---|
| Heath | 1/11 to 2/11 | | Demobilisation. No 1 Draft arriving Camp | |
| | 13/11 | | Lt Col Critchet returned from leave & took over Command | |
| | 14/11 | | Col Critchet handed in hand to Capt Blank | |
| | 15/11 | | took over Command of Battalion | |
| | | | Lt Col Critchet resumed Command | |
| | 2/11/19 | | Capt Bowen Argyl proceeded to UK for Disposal | |
| | 3/11/19 | | | |

Headquarters
116th Infantry Brigade

Herewith War Diary for
month of February 1919.

28.2.1919

JC
25th
for Lieut-Colonel
Northd. Fusiliers

Army Form C. 2118.

25 N F

76 58

# WAR DIARY
## or
## INTELLIGENCE SUMMARY.
*(Erase heading not required.)*

| Place | Date | Hour | Summary of Events and Information | Remarks and references to Appendices |
|---|---|---|---|---|
| Havre | Feb 1/28 1919 | | Demobilizing troops to U.K. from No 1 Despatching Camp Havre. Lt. Colonel A.H. Critchpole evacuated to Hospital sick. Captain G. Guly M.C M.M. assumed command of Battalion. | |
| " | Feb 19/1919 | | Capt A Blake reported back from leave + assumed duties of A/Adjutant vice Capt J Brownrit to U.K. demobilized. | |

25 N F

Vol 39

**WAR DIARY**
or
**INTELLIGENCE SUMMARY**

Army Form C. 2118.

| Place | Date | Hour | Summary of Events and Information | Remarks and references to Appendices |
|---|---|---|---|---|
| Hun | 1/3/19 to 31/5/19 | | Demobilizing Officers & others tanks from France, Salonica & other theatres of war. | |
| do | 14/3/19 | | Lt. Col. A.H. Catchpole rejoined Battalion from sick leave. | |

A. H. Catchpole Lieut Colonel
Comdg 25th Northd Fusiliers

**WAR DIARY**
or
**INTELLIGENCE SUMMARY.**

Army Form C. 2118.

2/5 NF

| Place | Date | Hour | Summary of Events and Information | Remarks and references to Appendices |
|---|---|---|---|---|
| Haarn | April 1-26 1919 | | Demobilising Officers & other Ranks to UK. | |
| | 26th | | Handed over Demobilisation duties to 18th Middlesex Regt at 12 noon | |
| | 27th to 30th | | Standing by to proceed to UK | |

Harold Cuffe(?)
Lieut. Colonel
2/5th Northd Fusiliers

www.ingramcontent.com/pod-product-compliance
Lightning Source LLC
Chambersburg PA
CBHW081244170426

43191CB00034B/2040